HOW DO BATS FLY IN THE DARK?

MELISSA STEWART

 **Marshall Cavendish**
Benchmark
New York

Marshall Cavendish Benchmark
99 White Plains Road
Tarrytown, NY 10591-5502
www.marshallcavendish.us

Library of Congress Cataloging-in-Publication Data

Stewart, Melissa.
How do bats fly in the dark? / by Melissa Stewart.
p. cm. — (Tell me why, tell me how)
Summary: "Provides comprehensive information on bats and the process of how they use their sensory system to find their way in the dark"—Provided by publisher.
Includes index.
ISBN 978-0-7614-2924-1
1. Bats—Juvenile literature. 2. Echolocation (Physiology) —Juvenile literature. I. Title.

QL737.C5S7446 2008
599.4'1479—dc22

2007023821

Photo research by Candlepants Incorporated

Cover Photo: BIOS Deschandol & Sabine Frank & Philippe / Peter Arnold Inc.

The photographs in this book are used by permission and through the courtesy of:
Peter Arnold Inc.: ullstein-Nill, 1, 12, 23; BIOS Allofs Theo, 4; Gunter Ziesler, 25. *Corbis*: Joe McDonald, 5; David A. Northcott, 22. *Photo Researchers Inc.*: Dr. Merlin D. Tuttle, 6; Habbick Visions, 8; Norden Cheatham, 10; Stephen Dalton, 13. *Getty Images*: Time & Life Pictures, 7; National Geographic, 11; Visuals Unlimited, 14; Aurora, 18; Photonica, 20. *Minden Pictures*: Jim Brandenburg, 15; Michael Durham, 17; Bruce Davidson, 19; Christian Ziegler, 24. *Animals Animals*: Stephen Dalton/OSF, 16.

Editor: Joy Bean
Publisher: Michelle Bisson
Art Director: Anahid Hamparian
Series Designer: Alex Ferrari

Printed in Malaysia
1 3 5 6 4 2

CONTENTS

Most bats hang upside down while they sleep. When they wake up, they climb to a high spot and fall into flight.

Two Kinds of Bats

Have you ever been playing outside on a summer evening and seen the jerky flight of "birds" above you? Chances are you were not really looking at birds. Those flitting creatures were probably bats.

Most birds are active during the day. By late afternoon, they are safely nestled in their sleeping spots. But most bats

Most bats are active at night and sleep during the day.

come out at night. As the sun goes down, they wake up and take flight.

Both birds and bats have wings. That is where their similarities end. Bats are **mammals**. They are more closely related to people than they are to birds.

No one knows exactly how many different kinds, or **species**, of bats live on Earth. So far, scientists have identified more than nine hundred species. But there may be more than that. Most bats are active at night, so they can be hard to track down.

This long-nosed bat uses its nose for finding nectar.

Scientists divide bats into two large groups: the **megabats** and the **microbats**. About 170 species of megabats live on Earth today. Nearly all of them live in warm, tropical places. Megabats are larger than microbats. They have larger eyes and smaller ears. Most megabats eat fruit, which they find with their sharp eyes and excellent sense of smell. They may also feed on the **nectar** and **pollen** of flowers.

Some megabats are active in the early morning and late afternoon. At the time most bats are flying out to feed, these megabats find a large tree and settle in for the night.

Microbats live all over the world. More than forty species of these small, nighttime fliers make their homes in the United States and Canada. Most of them **roost** in large groups called

There is no need for bug spray when microbats are around. These hungry hunters can eat more than one thousand insects an hour.

colonies. They spend their days hanging upside down in caves and other dark places.

Most microbats hunt insects, but some swoop down over water to snag fish or frogs. Three kinds of microbats drink the blood of other animals.

Microbats use their ears to "see" in the dark. They send out sounds and listen for the echoes the sounds make as they bounce off objects.

Microbats have smaller eyes than megabats, but they are not blind. Because microbats hunt insects and other moving targets, they rely on a sensory system

called **echolocation** to find their food. It is the perfect way to "see" in the dark.

As a microbat flies, it belts out a series of whistling calls. Its large ears pick up the echoes of those calls as they bounce off surrounding surfaces. The bat uses the echoes to judge the size, shape, and exact location of insects and other potential **prey**.

This short-tailed leaf-nosed bat's funny-looking nose acts as a megaphone. It blasts high-pitched calls into the night.

Sending Out Sounds

When you talk, the **larynx**, or voice box, in your throat is responsible for producing sounds. Bats have a larynx, too. Most of them use it to make their echolocation calls. A few bats, however, echolocate by making clicking noises with their tongue.

Many bats send out their echolocation sounds through their mouths. But some use their noses. These bats often have oddly shaped snouts. In many cases, a microbat's name hints at its unusual facial feature. There are long-nosed bats and short-nosed bats, spear-nosed bats and hammer-headed bats, leaf-nosed bats and slit-faced bats.

Some people think bats are blind. But megabats have excellent vision. They depend on their eyes and sense of smell to find nectar and fruit.

When a microbat flies, it directs its calls in a narrow path like the beam of a flashlight. As the bat turns its head from side to side, it changes the shape of its nose or mouth to alter the sounds it makes.

People can hear the echolocation calls that some bats make. But most bat cries are out of our hearing range. And that

Using echolocation, this microbat closes in on a moth.

is a good thing, because some bats are very loud.

Big brown bats and little brown bats usually hunt out in the open. Their high-volume whistles are as loud as a smoke detector held just 4 inches (10 centimeters) from one's ear. Bats that hunt in forests, however, usually make less noise. A northern long-eared bat's calls are about as loud as a person talking on the telephone in a normal voice.

Now I Know!

Why do some bats have large, strange-looking noses?

They use their noses to send out echolocation sounds.

How do the loudest bats constantly call out without going deaf? They switch their ears "off" just before belting out a call. Then they turn their ears back "on" before the first echoes arrive. What a great trick!

This false vampire bat has caught a mouse for dinner.

13

Bats are the only mammals to truly
fly. Flying squirrels and flying lemurs
can glide, but they cannot fly.

Echo, Echo, Echo

As a bat travels above a field or other open area, it sends out one or two calls each second. When the echoes arrive, they tell the bat how far away the ground is.

Many bats spend their nights flying through forests. In the woods, bats call out about ten times per second. The echoes help the bats "see" tree branches, rocks, and other objects that do not move. Bats send out sounds at about the same rate when they are moving around inside caves.

When microbats fly through the forest, they use echolocation to avoid bumping into trees.

At hunting time, a bat belts out a series of short, rapid calls. Because a microbat's prey is always on the move, the hunter needs constant input to pinpoint its meal. As a bat closes in for the kill, two hundred calls may pulse through the air each second.

A bat using echolocation can detect objects as small as a human hair. This bat has "spotted" a mouse on a branch.

Echolocation allows bats to find and catch prey in as little as half a second. At this rate, a bat can eat more than half its body weight in insects each night.

For echolocation to work, a bat needs ears that are perfectly in tune with its calls. Many microbats have large ears with wrinkles and folds that detect even the smallest sounds. They travel to the bat's brain, where the sounds form a picture of the animal's surroundings.

The system works so well that microbats have no trouble telling the difference between the steady beating of a moth's wings and the gentle fluttering of leaves. The quality of the sound tells a bat whether an object is big or small, flat or round, soft and smooth, or hard and rough.

To judge the exact location of an object, a bat listens to the difference in the echoes received by its left and right ears.

The hoary bat has thick fur with white tips. It lives in forests throughout the United States and Southern Canada.

To tell how far away the object is, the bat keeps track of the time between when it calls out and when the echo returns. If an object is nearby, the sound comes back quickly. If the object is farther away, the reflected sound takes longer to travel back to the bat's ear.

A bat's wings are lightweight and flexible. To change direction, a bat moves its long, thin fingers.

A Bat's Wings

Birds and bats both have wings, but their wings are built in different ways. A bird's rigid wings are supported by its arm bones. The hand and finger bones are **fused**, or joined together, for extra strength. A layer of lightweight feathers overlaps to cover the wings.

The bones that support a bat's wings are similar to the bones in a human arm and hand. But the arm bones are

In this close-up view of a bat's wing, you can see its long finger bones and tiny thumb.

A bat's back legs have tiny feet with long, sharp toenails. They are perfect for clinging to tree branches or cave walls.

much smaller, of course. The hand and finger bones are much longer and thinner. Instead of feathers, a bat's wings are covered with a leathery skinlike layer called the **patagium**. It is so thin that light can be seen through it. The patagium stretches between the bat's finger bones, giving the wing a weblike appearance. There is no flesh between the double-layered membrane—just bones, **nerves**, and **blood vessels**.

Unlike bird wings, bat wings are not rigid. The flexible fingers and stretchy skin allow bats to maneuver through the air like a stunt airplane. By moving its fingers ever so slightly, a bat can change direction at lightning speed. It can zip and zigzag, dip and dive, climb and tumble. It can even hover like a hummingbird.

Sometimes a microbat uses its flexible wings to capture moths and other flying insects. It flexes its fingers to make a scoop in its wing. Then the bat strikes the insect, grabs the stunned creature with its back feet, and pops the prey into its mouth.

Now I Know!
What is the patagium?

The leathery, skinlike material that covers a bat's wings.

Strong muscles in a bat's
back and chest help it
fly through the air.

How Do Bats Fly in the Dark?

As the sun goes down, a bat shakes itself awake and takes a look around. If the coast is clear, it drops into a free fall. But before the bat hits the ground, its wings take flight. It cruises out into the night and begins searching for food.

A bat flies by using its large back and chest muscles to flap its wings up and down. With every wing beat, the bat's long, thin finger bones adjust to take the bat where it wants to go.

Sometimes bats swoop close to the ground as they search for prey. They can quickly change their height or direction by moving their finger bones.

During each upstroke, one group of muscles pulls a bat's wings up. The animal folds its wings so it is easier to lift them through the air. On the down stroke, another group of muscles works to pull the bat's wings down. The force of its wings pressing against the air is what moves the bat forward.

After a long flight through the tropical rainforest, this megabat enjoys feasting on a fig.

Bats that hunt in open areas have long, thin wings. These help the nighttime hunters fly fast and straight. Bats that feed in forests have shorter, wider wings. This wing shape helps the bats weave around trees and other objects.

As a megabat flies, it uses its eyes and nose to find fruit. But microbats constantly call out into the night. With each returning echo, these bats get a more complete picture of their world. If a microbat spots a tree, it adjusts its wings to fly around it. And if it darts past a tasty insect, the bat uses its tail to put on the brakes. Then it quickly changes direction and chases after the prey.

After a full night of hunting, a bat returns to its roost. Just before landing, the bat does a quick flip. That way it lands

After spending many hours searching for food, it is time for this bat to take a rest.

Now I Know!

What pulls a bat's wings up and down as it flies?

Muscles.

hanging upside down. The bat folds its wings alongside its body like a collapsed umbrella. Then it drifts off to sleep.

Activity

Here is your chance to sense the world like a microbat. To do this experiment, you will need to go to a large courtyard with a high vertical wall. Ask your parents, teacher, or a local librarian for help finding one. You will need to bring a ruler or a meter stick, masking tape, a digital watch that measures seconds, a notebook, a pencil, and a friend.

1. Use the ruler or meter stick to find a spot 6.5 feet (20 meters) from the high courtyard wall. Mark the spot with masking tape. Now mark three other spots around the courtyard. One spot should be closer to the wall. One should be farther from the wall. One should be off to the side.

2. Stand on the first tape mark and clap your hands. You should hear a clear, sharp echo. This is

the sound of your clap bouncing off the wall and returning to your ears.

3. Start clapping at a rate of about two claps per second. Have your friend move around the courtyard to the other tape marks. Ask the friend to make notes about any differences he or she hears in the echoes at different locations.

4. Start clapping faster, but keep the rate steady. Have your friend listen at each of the tape marks again. Does he or she notice any differences? If so, write them down in the notebook.

5. Start clapping so fast that the claps and the echoes coincide. Have your friend count the number of claps you make in one second.

6. Now move to each of the other tape marks and repeat step five. Are the results different? If so, can you explain why?

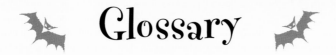Glossary

blood vessel—A tube that carries blood through the body.

colony—A large group of animals that sleeps and raises their young together.

echolocation—A sensory system that involves sending out sounds and listening to the returning echoes. Animals that echolocate can detect the size, distance, and texture of objects by interpreting the echoes.

fused—Joined together.

larynx—An organ in the throat that produces sounds.

mammal—A warm-blooded animal.

megabat—A large bat that lives in tropical areas, eats fruit, and usually does not use echolocation.

microbat—A small bat that can live anywhere in the world and hunts moving prey using echolocation.

nectar—A sugary liquid that many flowers produce. It attracts insects that spread the plant's pollen.

nerve—A cell or group of cells that carries messages to the brain.

patagium—The stretchy, skinlike layer that covers a bat's wings.

pollen—A sticky powder that must be spread from one flower to another in order for a plant to reproduce.

prey—An animal that is hunted by a predator.

roost—To rest or sleep (*verb*). A safe, quiet place where an animal rests or sleeps (*noun*).

species—A group of similar creatures that can mate and produce healthy young.

Find Out More

BOOKS

Davies, Nicola. *Bat Loves the Night*. Cambridge, MA: Candlewick, 2004.

Markle, Sandra. *Little Lost Bat*. Watertown, MA: Charlesbridge, 2006.

Markle, Sandra. *Outside and Inside Bats*. New York: Walker, 2004.

WEB SITES

Animal Bytes: Bats

http://www.seaworld.org/animal-info/animalbytes/animalia/eumetazoa/coelomates/deuterostomes/chordates/craniata/mammalia/chiroptera/bats.htm

From Sea World's Web site, fun facts about bats.

Bat Conservation International

http://www.batcon.org/home/default.asp

Lots of information about bats, including an extensive photo gallery, from an organization that strives to protect and conserve bat habitats.

Chiroptera: Night Fliers

http://www.ucmp.berkeley.edu/mammal/eutheria/chiroptera.html

A more scientific look at bats from the University of California Museum of Paleontology.

Encyclopedia Smithsonian: Bat Facts

http://www.si.edu/Encyclopedia_SI/nmnh/batfacts.htm

An overview of bats, from the Smithsonian Institution's Department of Systematic Biology.

Index

Page numbers for illustrations are in **boldface.**